Blueprint

Tia Jham

BookLeaf
Publishing

India | USA | UK

Dedication

To my parents, Amit and Kanchan, and my brother Neil

Preface

This anthology is crafted by those silent, introspective moments, where powerful feelings are reflected upon. Consisting of 21 poems, each one has a unique perspective on relatable themes about existence, and life around us.

I am a girl who finds solace in dreams and fantasies, and writing this book has always been merely a daydream. Letting my writing out into the world is truly an unexplainable feeling (even though I'm a writer) and I hope you feel the same passion as a reader, that I felt while composing each piece.

Acknowledgements

Firstly, thank you to my mother, my father, and my brother for being the wind beneath my wings and guiding me through this journey.

Thank you to Ms Sara Ghobadi - without who this would have never happened - for providing endless inspiration and helping me make a mere dream come true.

Thank you to my friends who were my biggest cheerleaders. And, to Sejal Aunty for the constant encouragement.

Magic

There is an unrecognised monotony in living
in a world of planning and justification.
Rather, I am hopelessly in love with a world
far vaster. For what is wrong with *'ifs'* and *'maybes'*?

A world where darkness is our fool, flowers
floating on summer rivers
and poetry that tears apart your soul.
But what use is poetry- when the rest of the world
cannot read?

You wouldn't care to understand what I have seen
in my own world, but quite frankly,
only if there is beauty in your mind
will you actually see it come alive.

Sunspills

'Cool'-
A place of darkness, where one's heart
starts to freeze over.
Consuming, like a sullen bouquet,
with wrinkles of past hardships.
A shield of protection, that eventually
becomes a part of oneself.

But as for me, I like to stay warm.

Where dreams are alive,
and joy thrives.
Where there's a home in your heart for
the people who endure the rain with you-
where there is a choice to be dry.
Warmth breeds new life:
a place where every lost item comes back to you,
and the whole world spins in a smooth jazz.

Stitching Dawn

Today, I came to buy a smile,
but what perplexed me is that it did not cost a penny,
or a timeworn jewel,
yet a price far cruel - Hope.

Hope is a frail, white thread - weaving together a better
fabric of tomorrow;
but just know, it is the one string that cannot be cut,
rather, merely lost.

I asked the seller, where this Hope may be
but he simply told me,
'Chase it, and it ceases.'

Dreaming tides

My dreams are painted in colours that do not yet exist, but
oh, the unfair proximity of ambition; an echo
from another time; another place. Coming
in waves - froth-chained; pouncing; passionate.
The storm in my chest is 'perfectly ruined' draped in
blue -
but tonight, my winged ideas are drowning.

Once, I voyaged to find these waves; hungry lions;
where the sky meets the sun; the line converging cold
darkness
and burning passion. Yet, I discovered that the tides
shifted beneath me, and
again, I was adrift in the boundless blue.

Until the sunrise.

Head in the Clouds

I built my sanctuary of clouds
brick-by-brick,
above somber plains and
beneath the Divine's heavenly embrace.

It has wall-to-wall billowing clouds,
accompanied by soaring, Greek columns of sunbeams
and an arching roof of Dawn's mists;
with the scent of Spring's arrival.
Where breezes like swift serpents inhabit,
and nightingales of varied hues serenade
my house in the clouds- with their sonorous melodies.

But one day, the clouds shall burst open
with a torrential downpour and
my house will crumble.
What remains will be
the house of clouds in my mind -
where dreams roam free.

Epiphany

I see the lanterns in my mind
and when the day comes that I see them no more,
I know that they burn - eternal.
This is what we are - crafted in the knowing that
the lanterns forever beam;
all you need to do is blink and they shall appear.

Swirling branches, trees in passionate colours.
Stardust, yearning to go home.
Worlds light years away.
For that is where we belong -

We do not belong here, we belong in realms
of passion; intensity and ambition.
We are inmates; lurkers; puppets.
Trapped within it all.

We are explorers. Pioneers;
in existence to overcome the impossible.
Generations of humanity weaving together a better
tomorrow,
building the monuments of the future.
But oh, Rome only takes one day to burn
and the light can vanish in seconds.

The secret is, surround yourself with people
who make your heart smile;
only then will you truly ignite your lanterns.

Masquerade

Isn't it baffling how we're all pretending?
Pretending to be normal, when we could paint the world
in our rich colours; accents; and tales.
'Normal' is a construct, just like time,
and one day, you will lay in the graveyard of your
heritage:
hoping; longing; yearning that you had embraced
yourself -
unmasked, while you still could.

But the seats are empty.
The theatre is dark.
Why do we keep acting?
The play must go on - right?
What is your role if your verse isn't yours?

Who are you?

I see us all in our distinct gowns, with
our shades woven into tapestries of tulle.
But when the knowing rain unleashes its torrential
forces,
our riot of colour fades and masks slip off.

We walk through the storm, timid -
but what if the storm was ours to create?

Bloodlines

India is a fighter,
seizing her incessant meanders
alongside screeching mountains
and whispering valleys.

India's red saree drapes across nine yards,
with the relentless blood of her daughters.
Their wings are clipped; their feet are tied
like caged birds.
The borders of their sarees are invaded -
as if her daughters are property to be colonised
by repulsive desires.
Shrieking.
Yet they remain silenced- as predatory lust consumes
men. Their
grips tighten around the daughters' feeble throats,
feeling their heartbeat wane.

Maybe these women are unable
to yelp, while they bleed across nine yards.
But, I will pick out my own song of freedom from this
uproar;
and at last, I will throw my head back and sing it,
to embellish their crimson sarees with traces of blue.

What Once Was

There we sat: watching the sun's embrace
on the horizon, as its golden petals
seeped into the rich azure space.
Sparks.

There we sat: while treasure ever so bright
at the end of the rainbow, our minds
like bookshelves, holding dreams so tight.
Flames.

tick.
tock.

The endless continuum: wilting flowers
once flourishing.
Ashes.

When swallowed by the sea, my lighthouse
beams; watching me sink with the
Weight of emptiness.
scars.

My mosaic dwells locked in my chest:
with my moments in all their colours;

even the rather morose ones.
There you were:
unsullied...

Crack -
A shattered shard.

  a blank space.

Again, *there* I sat,
wondering... if the Gods enjoy watching
my entire World burn.

The Prize

Ten years old, Aurora chased
fireflies like fallen stars, in the twilight.
Her grandfather, Otto, watched her on the porch swing
with a radiating smile. Time etched lines on his face,
a map of the years he'd traversed.

"Aurora catch one!" he exclaimed.
She leapt with the thrill of the chase yet
the firefly disappeared into thin air.
She shrugged, "They're too quick Grandpa."
"Just like time, my dear."
"But what *is* time Grandpa?"

"Aurora, time is a rich language, which helps
you understand the ancient tales of our universe.
There may be a few words you are unfamiliar with,
but in the end, it will all be forgotten."

A frown settled on Aurora's face. The idea of losing
this vibrant world, and catching fireflies,
perplexed the knowing child.
Otto held her hand, "It is all a prize, but only a matter of
time
until you see it."

One summer evening after she turned sixteen, Aurora
returned to the same porch.
"Remember the fireflies, Grandpa?" she asked,
with a tinge of nostalgia,
"How could I forget," his weak smile tugged the corner of
his eyes,
"But what is the prize?"
"It's only a matter of time until you see it Aurora..."

After her grandfather's passing,
Aurora returned to the porch
as she sought an oasis to let her darkness
take refuge. The sky was dimmer,
the fireflies had fled and stars faded
into the void of ebony. But as she sat
on the swing, she felt the gentlest touch of warmth.
The prize was yet uncertain, but she had
won the jackpot by once having Otto in her life-

And just as she reminisced, she saw a faint
glimmer of light:
a *firefly*.

Crying Moments

Have you ever encountered a moment,
deeply planted in the grave soils of your life,
crying out to flourish before you?

Like: when you talk to the world, telling others
about their incomparable beauty. Or, letting
your love fall like gentle rain wherever
your footsteps grace.

Or, when moments scrape through your fingers;
a bittersweet farewell. When your heart sinks
through sullen shades with the weight of what could be -
and what never would be again.

But just remember, if a snake bites you,
rather than asking why it bit you;
or if you deserve it;
heal the venom and come out with a newfound strength.
And just know, it was sent as a sign
from beyond -

Lost

Dear Old Me,
I wish I could tell you
that I have never stopped bringing flowers
to your grave.
Clinging to lasting memories, your imaginary friend
has aged with your thoughts- fading; hiding; subsiding...

Take me home today, but not to *this* one.
Take me to the home where my brother and I
chased each other 'round the kitchen each day;
where Dad taught me to ride a bike and Mom
to bake.
Take me home to yesterday.

But Dear Old Me,
Please leave your light on,
so I can find my way back to you.

Pretty Enough

They tell us to be
'Pretty.'
But never outshine another girl,
'Look at those models, be like them'-
but blind the tears rolling down your cheek
with layers, and layers of makeup -
since your appearance can be hidden beyond filters too.
Though, ensure not to put on too much makeup
to look 'natural' but not too little, so that
you look tired.
There are steps to the process,
which just keep towering;
and when you reach the top, it's
just as lonely as it was at the bottom.
Plastered smiles smeared across faces -
as if we're surgical projects,
but just know that you will only look your best
when you're bleeding on the inside.
'Maintain it, no matter it the cost.'

What am I maintaining?

A lie. A fantasy.

A fantasy that is finally pretty,
but never pretty *enough*.

If Mirrors Could Talk...

They would see generations, tearing
themselves apart over fractures uncertain that could be
seen, nonetheless felt so deeply. They would see you
closing your eyes,
longing inside for more-

They would disclose that your appearance is a decorated
doorway, which
surely should look inviting. However, after you enter the
doorway,
there is no memory of the door itself; simply intentions
to make oneself feel at home.

They would confess that anyone can learn to love
a rose. Those fragrant poems painted with
scarlet; a timeless beauty. But what of the
leaves that embellish? Those that give
this world life, the reason for you and I, yet
perceived as wasted potential. Intricate
venation, echoing beauty that
the rose cannot be grasped by its thorns.

Housewarming

Dear friend, I come bearing a gift of grief.
Let it enter your home,
ripping your insides to tatters,
and let it flow through you like a soft, murky river.

Wrapped in red ribbon, I bring a gift of heartache;
ignited by curious, sinister melodies.
Voids crying out to be fulfilled
and your pulse beating away at sea.

Do not forget to entertain sorrow!
A pain like decaying teeth, only to adorn
your jaw with shiny, new embellishments.
But I warn you, do not wrap this gift up and send it
along.

Surely, invite them all to be the air that inhabits you -
embrace them, as they open up your tinted windows,
clearing up the darkness for a new warmth;
letting the light pour in-
while their sunrays point to destiny.

Sonnet to the Sun

Isn't there an obscured beauty in the Sun
forever giving its light to the Moon, and never
asking for anything in return?
It burns below the heavens with flames
of passion, igniting a healing joy
and dissipating its fervour all around.
Casting its solemn stares upon me,
it stands alone; desolate; forlorn-
with its constant friend of loneliness.
Tirelessly, it blazes: yearning for times of stillness-
to catch a breath, and watch the world pass by.
It wonders why it is surrounded by darkness,
and I pray that someday,
the Sun realises that it is the Light that brightens us all.

Views

Time is a windowsill that I gaze out of,
and I see the world quivering around me,
with surface-level lust; jealousy; and unrequited love,
I listen to wise men in anguish
at ashen dreams and tattered ambition,
I taste murk-bound tears, as loved ones turn to dust-
and houses full of life are dappled with Death,
I touch splintered mosaics, like laying in a
field of bygones - with the bittersweet flavour
of homesickness,
so, I search the darkness for traces of light.

But I can smell vivid pastures with defiant tulips -
and Spring's arrival.
While the World longs for God's identity papers,
if you gaze out of the windowsill, you just might find
them.

Autumn

Autumn is the ginger girl with auburn hair
cascading down her back like liquid copper.
Her chest is hollow, but weighted
with a metronome-like ticking and twinges in her heart
with the ghosts of summer. Upon her descent
comes sun-dappled shades of amber,
pouring into empty churches; silent tears; and
a torn page from a poet's book.
She smells like warm honey, the texture of luxurious
velvet and shows us
the Art of letting go.

Wandering Paper Boats

Once, I journeyed
upon myriad shores where sandcastles soared to the
lofty
peaks of my dreams. Bottomless pits once dug
with shovels of fossilised colours, searching; finding;
digging;
without a worry that the tide would wash
everything away.

My voyage weaved the tapestry
of my existence, halting at a bridge, like
the Lego set mother bought me for my thirteenth
birthday. But this,
was indistinct: blending; fading- like the lyrics to a
forgotten
melody.

But here I am - adrift in large, imperious waves:
no compass; no land in sight; just my lonesome -
knowing that a day shall arrive when the tide soaks me
under.

Even when it does, my voyage of the tides

will be whispered in the ancient lore of the waves-
or yet another shipwreck.

The World of Literature

A packed passport, longing for a space;
a breath. But to wander, the fear of
never quite finding oneself between the in-betweens.
The fear of the nights, staring at your ceiling,
remembering what will be forgotten. The fear of forever,
lasting all but a heartbeat.

Soon the monsters below my bed shall be my comrades,
and
I see my fears are seldom alone. That only in my mind
shall I ever
be lonesome, for I belong in the world where every
word;
every phrase is etched into the soul:
The world of literature.

The Price of Poetry

Why do I write to you, dear poem, if you never reply?
I write for the day that these leaves are held,
and someone from somewhere
picks my soul off of your venation.
For that is what you are dear poem, with your
stems branching out, and your layered nuances,
providing
greenery in this void of darkness.
Why do I write to you, dear poem, if one day,
someone from somewhere finds that it is them carved
in your veins?
But, that is a price I am willing to pay
for even if you wilt, my words shall stay.